In Touch with Science

What is Energy?

Richard and Louise Spilsbury

W
FRANKLIN WATTS
LONDON·SYDNEY

This edition first published in 2009 by
Franklin Watts
338 Euston Road
London NW1 3BH

Franklin Watts Australia
Level 17/207 Kent Street
Sydney, NSW 2000

First published in 2008 by Enslow Elementary
an imprint of Enslow Publishers, Inc.

Copyright © 2008
The Brown Reference Group plc

A CIP catalogue record for this book is available from
the British Library.

ISBN 978 0 7496 8420 4

Dewey Decimal Classification Number 531'.6

Photographic and Illustration Credits:
Illustrations by Geoff Ward. Model Photography by Tudor
Photography. Additional photographs from istockphoto,
pp. 18, 24; Science Photo Library, p. 6; Shutterstock,
pp. 4, 8, 14, 18, 22.

Cover Photo: Tudor Photography

Every attempt has been made to clear copyright.
Should there be any inadvertent omission please
apply to the publisher for rectification.

For The Brown Reference Group plc
Project Editor: Sarah Eason
Designer: Paul Myerscough
Picture Researcher: Maria Joannou
Managing Editor: Bridget Giles
Editorial Director: Lindsey Lowe
Production Director: Alastair Gourlay
Children's Publisher: Anne O'Daly

Printed in Malaysia

Franklin Watts is a division of
Hachette Children's Books,
an Hachette Livre UK Company.
www.hachettelivre.co.uk

contents

WHAT IS ENERGY?

Birds fly, people walk and computer screens glow. They all use energy.

Energy is the ability to do work, for example to make something move or change. Energy comes in many different forms. Heat, light, sound and electricity are just a few forms of energy that we use every day.

Movement and Stored Energy

Some forms of energy involve movement. The scientific name for energy related to movement is kinetic energy.

Things that do not move can also have energy. They have stored energy, or potential energy. A plastic cup of water resting on the edge of a table has potential energy because it could fall. If you knock the cup off the table, it moves towards the ground.

CLOSE-UP

SPRINGS

When you press down on a spring, it gains potential energy. If you let go, the spring will leap back into shape.

You put energy into the spring when you press it. The spring stores the energy, and then releases it as kinetic energy when you let go.

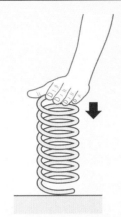

- A hand uses energy to push on a spring. That energy changes to potential energy as the spring coils tighten.

- The potential energy changes into kinetic energy as the spring leaps up.

◀ *The billboards use energy in the form of electricity which creates heat and light.*

The cup's potential energy becomes kinetic energy. Stretched elastic bands and coiled springs have potential energy.

Changing Energy

Once energy has made something happen, the energy is not destroyed and does not disappear. Instead, it changes form. For example, when a light is switched on, the electrical energy from the switch changes form into light and heat energy within the light bulb.

HEAT ENERGY

Heat is a very important form of energy. We use heat to cook our food and to keep our homes warm. But heat also affects many other things!

How much heat energy an object has depends on how much the atoms inside it move. Matter is made up of tiny particles called atoms. Atoms are joined together in different combinations, called molecules. Different kinds of atoms and molecules make up the different substances in the universe.

Heat Energy and Atoms

All atoms in an object constantly vibrate. However, atoms are so small that they and their movements can only be seen with a powerful microscope.

CLOSE-UP

HEAT AND STATES

Matter can exist in different states, such as solid, liquid or gas. Atoms or molecules in a solid are held closely together. They are held more loosely in a liquid, and in a gas they are widely spread.

Changes in heat energy can make substances change state. For example, solid ice melts into liquid water when heated. That happens because the molecules break away from each other and move more freely. When water becomes very hot, its molecules can also move more freely. Water then becomes a gas called water vapour.

● Solid molecules.

● Liquid molecules.

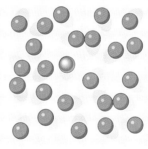
● Gas molecules.

◀ *Some machines show heat energy. This is a thermogram image of a baby. The red areas show where the heat energy in its body is strongest.*

Atoms move more when they are heated up. The more an object is heated up (the more heat energy it has) the faster its atoms will vibrate. The vibrating of the atoms themselves causes an increase in temperature. The hotter something is, the more its atoms move, and the more kinetic energy its atoms have.

MOVING HEAT

If you stand near an oven or put your hand a few centimetres above a radiator, you will feel heat. This is because heat energy moves from the radiator towards you.

Heat energy usually travels from hotter objects to cooler ones. It keeps moving until the two objects become the same temperature. For instance, if a hot pan is left on a table, the pan will cool down until it is the same temperature as the table and the air around it.

Conduction

The way in which heat moves through solid materials is called conduction. When a teaspoon is placed in hot water, the atoms in the spoon start to vibrate quickly. These atoms knock into their neighbouring atoms, which makes them move faster, too. This process makes heat pass up to the top of the spoon.

CLOSE-UP

CONVECTION CURRENTS

Convection makes heat move through liquids and gases. In a pan of water on a hot stove, the water molecules closest to the heat move faster and take up more space than the colder water above. Since the hot water is now less dense, it rises above the cold water.

The cold water beneath the hot water is now warmed by the stove. The warm water at the top cools as it passes energy to the cold air at the surface. The warm water then gets denser and sinks again. All the water eventually reaches the same temperature.

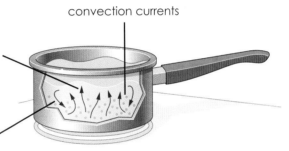

convection currents

Warm water rises above cold water as it becomes less dense.

Warm water at the surface becomes cooler and denser. It sinks to the bottom of the pan again.

A coat traps air next to a body. Air is not a good heat conductor. Instead, air traps the heat energy created by our bodies. So, body heat cannot escape into the cold air around us. In this way, coats help keep us warm.

Radiation

Heat can also move by radiation. Invisible rays of heat energy radiate, or spread outwards, from hot objects. The main source of heat energy on Earth is radiation from our nearest star, the Sun.

9

Make a Solar Oven

Can radiation cook a marshmallow? Follow these simple steps to find out.

SAFETY TIP

Ask an adult to make the holes in the cardboard.

1 Use the compass to draw a semi-circle roughly in the middle of each long edge of the box. Ask an adult to cut out the two semi-circle curves.

2 Place a piece of cardboard across the box, in the curves. Make pencil marks on each side of the cardboard where it fits into the curves. Cut the cardboard into one long strip that will fit inside the curves.

You will need

- shoebox bottom ● compass and pencil ● scissors
- cardboard ● aluminium foil ● masking tape
- wooden skewer
- marshmallows ● glue

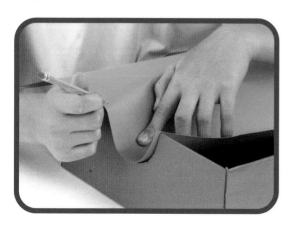

3 Use glue to stick the aluminium foil to the cardboard, keeping the foil shiny side out. Tape the foil-covered cardboard into the curve of the box.

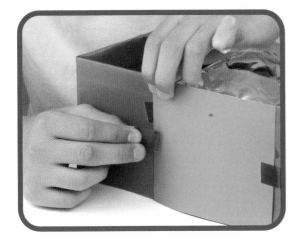

WHAT HAPPENED?

The shiny, curved cardboard reflected the Sun's rays directly on to the marshmallows. The heat energy carried by this radiation passed into the marshmallows. The rising temperature made the molecules inside the marshmallows move so much that the solid marshmallow changed state into a sticky liquid.

4 Cut two squares of cardboard to fit over each semi-circular hole. Ask an adult to make a small hole in each square, in the middle near the top. Use tape to stick the cardboard squares over the semi-circles in the box.

5 Push a wooden skewer through the hole in one side of the box. Push the skewer through a few marshmallows, and then push it through the hole in the other side of the box. Put the box outside in sunlight and watch the marshmallows melt!

Make a Convection Tank

Can convection currents be seen?
Try this experiment to find out.

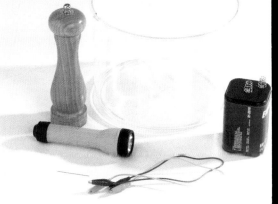

SAFETY TIP

Ask an adult to help with the experiment.
Do not let the battery touch the water.

1 Attach one crocodile clip from each electrical wire to either end of the pencil lead.

2 Attach the other end of one wire to the positive terminal on the battery (marked with +). Attach the other end of the second wire to the negative terminal (marked with –).

You will need

- 5 cm long lead from a mechanical pencil • two electrical wires with crocodile clips • small fish tank
- 6 volt battery • torch
- cool tap water • large piece of white posterboard • pepper

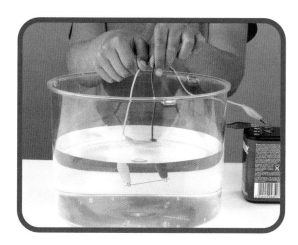

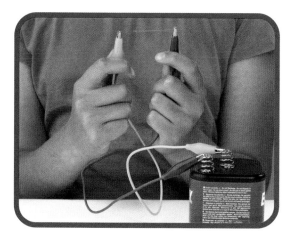

3 Fill the tank with cool tap water. Place the pencil lead into the water, but do not let it touch the sides.

4 Rest the posterboard against a pile of books beside the tank. Ask an adult to darken the room and shine a torch through the tank. The water's movement should be projected onto the cardboard.

5 If you cannot darken the room, you can see the movement of the water by grinding black pepper into it. The pepper flakes will move along with the water.

Try this!

Try the same experiment with a 12 volt battery. What happens?

WHAT HAPPENED?

Electricity from the battery flowed through the wire and the pencil lead. The electricity heated up the lead and warmed the water around the lead.

The warm water rose upwards, and was replaced by cooler water. The cooler water then also heated up and rose upwards. Convection currents were created. These were seen as light and dark patterns on the posterboard.

CHEMICAL ENERGY

Chemical energy is a form of potential energy. It can change into other types of energy, such as kinetic energy, heat, sound, light or electricity.

Chemical energy can be found in the arrangement of molecules in candle wax. When a candle is lit, its molecules are rearranged and their chemical energy changes into heat and light energy. When fireworks explode, their chemical energy is converted into a colourful display of light, sound and heat energy.

Releasing Chemical Energy

A chemical reaction happens when the molecules or atoms of one substance join with those of another. For example, iron slowly reacts with oxygen gas in the air or in water to make iron oxide (rust). This process releases chemical energy.

Burning

Burning is a common chemical reaction. It happens when a substance quickly reacts with oxygen and releases heat energy. Energy is stored in some materials that can be burnt. These materials are described as fuels. Wood, coal and oil are examples of fuels. They have lots of chemical energy, burn easily and release a lot of heat energy.

CLOSE-UP

FIREWORKS

The chemicals in fireworks create their special colours, patterns and sounds. The first chemical to burn in a firework is fuel. That releases a gas that forces the firework into the air. The firework now has kinetic energy.

Other chemicals burn when the firework is in the sky, creating colourful lights and loud sounds. For example, showers of blue stars form when chemicals that contain copper burn.

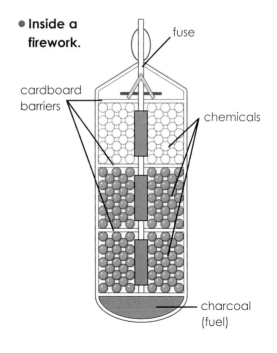

● **Inside a firework.**

fuse

cardboard barriers

chemicals

charcoal (fuel)

▲ *The engines of an aeroplane burn fuel. That creates exhaust gases that force the aeroplane forwards. The plane now has kinetic energy.*

Erupt a Volcano!

Did you know that you can make a volcano? Find out how!

You will need

- paper plate • small plastic bottle (such as a cola bottle) • modelling clay
- twigs and plastic figures • clean, dry funnel
- baking soda (about 3–4 tablespoons)
- glitter • 100ml vinegar • few drops of washing-up liquid • newspaper • water
- red food colouring • measuring jug

1 Stand the bottle in the centre of the plate. Use modelling clay to make a volcano shape around the sides of the bottle.

2 Decorate the volcano – you could use small twigs to look like trees.

3 Put the funnel in the top of the bottle and carefully spoon in the baking soda. Add the washing-up liquid and about 100 ml water. Add half a teaspoon of glitter.

4 Measure out 100 ml of vinegar and five drops of food colouring.

TIP

This is messy!
Wear old clothes
and protect the
work surface
with newspaper.

WHAT HAPPENED?

When vinegar was added to the bottle a chemical reaction began. The vinegar reacted with the baking soda to produce water, a chemical called sodium acetate and lots of carbon dioxide gas.

The carbon dioxide was trapped in bubbles of washing-up liquid in the water, making the water foam. There was not enough room in the bottle to contain the foam. Red colouring and glitter mixed with the foam. When the foam spurted from the bottle, it looked like lava.

5 Add the vinegar mix to the bottle. Quickly remove the funnel, and watch the eruption happen!

17

ENERGY FOR LIFE

Plants and animals need energy to live and grow. They get their energy from their food. The source of all the energy in food comes from the Sun.

Green plants are producers. This means they can collect light energy from the Sun through their leaves. They then use it to change water and carbon dioxide into food. This process is called photosynthesis. Plants store the sugary food that they produce inside their leaves and stems.

Food Chains

Green plants and seaweeds use photosynthesis to capture the Sun's energy. A rabbit is an example of a herbivore, a plant-eating animal. A fox is an example of a carnivore, a flesh-eating animal. Foxes get their energy from eating animals, including rabbits.

CLOSE-UP

MAKING FOSSIL FUELS

When coal is burned it releases energy that plants captured from the Sun about 300 million years ago! These fossil fuels, such as coal, are formed from the remains of plants that died millions of years ago. The dead plants were buried in mud. Then, over a very long period, they were pressed together and heated by heavy layers of rock. Gradually, the plants turned into coal.

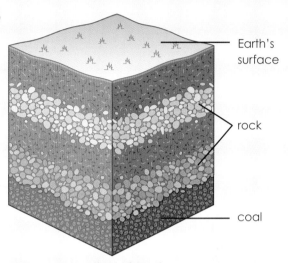

Earth's surface

rock

coal

● **A cross-section of Earth.**

This network of energy links between plants and animals is called a food chain. In any habitat there are many different food chains.

This caterpillar, bird and plant are part of a food chain. The caterpillar eats the plant, and the bird eats the caterpillar.

Using Food Energy

When an animal eats green plants or meat, its body turns the chemical energy in food into different types of chemicals. The animal's body uses some of these chemicals to make its muscles move, to keep warm or to repair and grow body parts. It also stores some of the chemicals to use later to make energy.

19

Build a Biosphere

What happens when you create a food chain? Try these simple steps to find out.

SAFETY TIP

Ask an adult to get the mud from the bottom of the pond. Make sure they wear rubber gloves to do it.

1 Ask an adult to make a hole in the jar lid. Cover the hole with a piece of wax, but remove it once a day to release any gases that build up inside.

2 Fill the jar two-thirds with pond water. Add 1.25 cm of mud.

You will need

- clean 1 litre jar with a screwtop lid
- wax • pond or lake water • mud from the bottom of a pond • water plants from an aquarium (such as elodea) • water snails (from a garden centre) • note pad and pen

3 Gently put some elodea or other small water plants in the jar. Add large water plants and the water snails.

4 Put the lid on the jar. Keep it somewhere cool, and where there is a little shade.

5 Make notes about the jar contents over the next few weeks. Record the colour of the water and the amount of light passing through the jar (for example, write down whether it is sunny or shady). Write down any changes that take place. When you have finished making your observations, gently empty the contents of the jar back into the pond.

WHAT HAPPENED?

A biosphere is a world that holds life. You created a miniature biosphere inside your jar. One of the changes you should have noticed in your biosphere was that the water became clearer. This happened because the plants took up nutrients from the water. Tiny eggs in the mud may also have hatched out into very small creatures that feed on nutrients in the water.

ELECTRICAL ENERGY

Electrical energy is used in many ways. It can create heat, light, movement or even sound.

Electrical energy changes into heat energy in an oven. It changes into sound and light energy in a television. Motors in washing machines and food processors convert electrical energy into motion energy.

Electrical Charges

All atoms have electrical charges, because they contain tiny particles called electrons. Electrons sometimes move between atoms. When electrons leave an atom, the atom becomes positively charged. When an atom gains electrons, it becomes negatively charged. Negative and positive charges attract each other. This causes electrons to flow between atoms. This is electricity.

Parts of an atom.

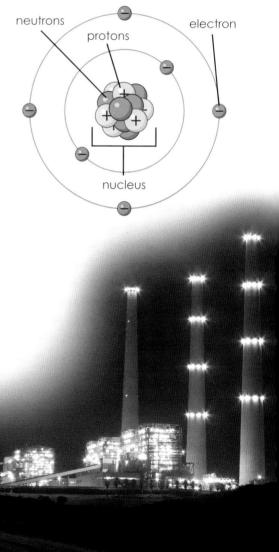

neutrons

protons

electron

nucleus

Electricity on the Move

When electrical charges keep flowing between atoms, they create an electrical current – the type of electricity that travels through cables and wires. Electrical currents are carried through materials called conductors. Electricity conductors are usually metal wires. The conductors must form a complete circuit, or circle, through which the current can flow.

Batteries

Batteries supply machines with small amounts of electrical energy, without the need to plug the machines into electrical sockets. Batteries do not contain electricity. Instead, they store chemical energy. When they are placed in a machine, they complete a circuit. The chemicals in them then react together to create electrical energy.

◀ *Inside a power station, a machine called a generator makes electricity for homes and other buildings.*

CLOSE-UP

LIGHTNING STRIKES

Lightning is a form of static electricity. People sometimes feel static electricity as a shock when they touch a door handle after walking across a carpet. Static electricity occurs when electrons rub off one substance and move on to another. Ice crystals and dust inside clouds rub against each other to create the static electricity in lightning.

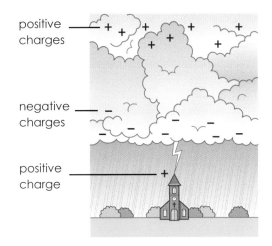

positive charges

negative charges

positive charge

- A flash of lightning occurs when a negatively charged spark jumps across a cloud.

- Lightning flashes also happen when negative charges in a cloud are attracted to positive charges on the ground.

RENEWABLE ENERGY

Renewable energy does not run out.
It is made from natural forms of energy,
such as wind, water and sunlight.

Fossil fuels are not renewable sources of energy because they will run out one day. Three-quarters of all the electrical energy used in the world today comes from burning fossil fuels, such as oil, coal and gas.

Water Power

In many parts of the world, people use the kinetic energy of moving water to make electricity. For example, water that flows down mountains is channelled into pipes that carry it through machines called turbines. The water spins the turbines. The turbines turn generators to create electricity produced by water, which is called hydro-electric power.

CLOSE-UP

SOLAR CELLS

Solar power is electricity that is made by using energy from the Sun. Solar panels collect the Sun's energy. The panels are made up of many solar cells. Each cell is a thin layer of silicon that lies next to a thinner layer of a slightly different material. When light hits the silicon layer, electrons from the second layer travel up to the silicon layer. This flow of electrons creates electricity.

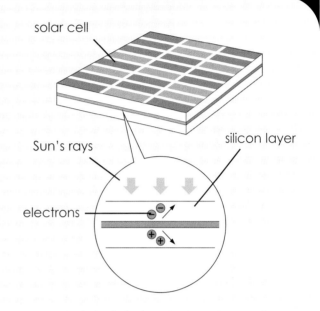

• **A cross-section of a solar cell.**

◀ *Renewable sources of electrical energy, such as these wind turbines, usually create very little pollution.*

Wind Power

Wind is moving air. To capture wind energy, turbines are built in windy places such as the tops of hills or out at sea. Wind turbines are tall towers with three or four blades. The wind makes the blades turn, like a propeller. The spinning blades then turn a generator to make electricity. A group of wind turbines is called a wind farm.

Making Sparks!

How is an electrical spark made? Try this experiment to find out.

You will need

- scissors • polystyrene tray
- masking tape • aluminium foil tray

1 Cut an L-shape from the polystyrene tray. Tape the L-shape to the centre of the foil tray to make a handle.

2 Rub the bottom of the polystyrene tray on your head, moving it quickly over your hair.

3 Place the polystyrene tray upside down on a table. Pick up the aluminium tray by its handle. Hold it about 30 cm above the tray, then drop it on to the tray.

WHAT HAPPENED?

The polystyrene tray became negatively charged when it was rubbed on your head. When the aluminium tray was put on the polystyrene, the electrons in the polystyrene repelled the electrons in the foil. The electrons leaped to your hand when you touched the foil. That made a spark.

The aluminium was positively charged when it was lifted from the polystyrene. Electrons jumped to the foil from your finger. That made another spark.

4 Gently touch the aluminium tray. You should feel a spark! (Do not touch the polystyrene tray.)

5 Use the handle to pick up the aluminium tray. Touch it again. You should feel another spark.

Try this!

Try this activity in a dark room. You should see tiny sparks when you touch the aluminium tray. What colour are they?

Make a Water Turbine

Can you harness the energy in moving water? Follow these steps to find out.

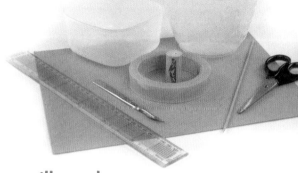

SAFETY TIP

Ask an adult to help you with this activity.

You will need

- jug of water • sticky tape • scissors
- wooden skewer • cork • cardboard
- ruler • sharp knife
- plastic ice cream container

1 Ask an adult to cut out 5 cardboard strips about 4 cm long and 2.5 cm wide.

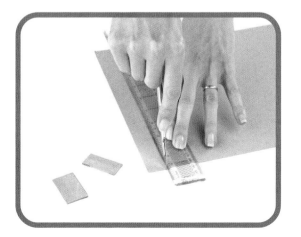

2 Ask the adult to make a hole through the centre of the cork, wide enough to push the skewer through. Then tape the cardboard strips onto the side of the cork.

WHAT HAPPENED?

As water poured over the cardboard strips, the potential energy in the water was converted into kinetic energy. That made the turbine move around, or spin. In a power station, the spinning of a turbine is used to create electrical energy.

3 Finally, ask an adult to make a hole in either side of the plastic container. Push the skewer through one hole, then through the hole in the cork and the other hole in the container.

4 The skewer should now be held in place in the centre of the container. You have made a water turbine! Pour water from the jug on to the cardboard strips. What happens?

GLOSSARY

atoms – Small particles that make up matter. Atoms contain even smaller particles called protons, neutrons and electrons.

biosphere – Contained environment that supports life.

circuit – Path in which an electrical current flows.

conduction – Process by which heat moves through solid objects.

convection – Process by which heat moves through liquids and gases.

electricity – The flow of electrons between atoms.

electron – Particle that moves around the nucleus (centre) of an atom. An electron has a negative electrical charge.

energy – Ability to do work, such as to make something move or change.

fossil fuel – Fuel made from the remains of plants and animals.

kinetic energy – The energy a moving object has because it is moving.

molecules – Groups of atoms joined together to form different kinds of matter.

neutron – Tiny particle found in the centre (nucleus) of an atom. Neutrons do not have a charge; they are neutral.

nutrients – Chemicals that living bodies use to help them function and grow.

photosynthesis – Process by which plants use light to make food from water and carbon dioxide.

potential energy – Energy that is stored in an object and ready to be used.

proton – Tiny particle found in the centre (nucleus) of an atom. Protons have a positive charge.

radiation – Movement of energy through air in waves or rays.

solar power – Electricity made using the energy from sunlight.

turbine – Machine with blades attached to a central rotating shaft. Turbines are used to generate electricity.

FURTHER READING

Books

Action for the Environment: Energy Supplies by Chris Oxlade,
    Franklin Watts, 2004, 2006
Improving our Environment: Saving Energy by Jen Green,
    Wayland, 2005, 2007
Our World: Future Energy by Rob Bowden, Franklin Watts, 2008
Science Alive: Energy by Chris Oxlade and Terry Jennings,
    Franklin Watts, 2008

Internet Addresses

To find out more about energy, play games and take quizzes, visit:
http://www.sciencemuseum.org.uk/on%2Dline/energy/

To find out more about saving energy, visit:
http://www.eere.energy.gov/kids/
http://www.energyquest.ca.gov/index.html/

INDEX